AMERICAN

MELANCHOLY

POETRY BY JOYCE CAROL OATES

Women in Love and Other Poems (1968)

Anonymous Sins and Other Poems (1969)

Love and Its Derangements (1970)

Angel Fire (1973)

Dreaming America (1973)

The Fabulous Beasts (1975)

Season of Peril (1977)

Women Whose Lives Are Food, Men Whose Lives Are Money (1978)

Invisible Woman: New and Selected Poems, 1970–1982 (1982)

The Time Traveler (1989)

Tenderness (1996)

AMERICAN

MELANCHOLY

POEMS

JOYCE CAROL OATES

An Imprint of HarperCollins*Publishers*

HarperCollins books may be purchased for educational, business, or sales promotional use. For information, please email the Special Markets Department at SPsales@harpercollins.com.

Ecco® and HarperCollins® are trademarks of HarperCollins Publishers.

FIRST EDITION

Designed by Michelle Crowe

Library of Congress Cataloging-in-Publication Data has been applied for.

ISBN 978-0-06-303526-3

21 22 23 24 25 LSC 10 9 8 7 6 5 4 3 2 1

For my poet-friend Henri Cole; and in memoriam,
Charlie Gross, first reader and beloved husband

CONTENTS

_____

III.

AMERICAN MELANCHOLY

IV.

"THIS IS THE TIME . . ."

AMERICAN

MELANCHOLY

I.

THE COMING STORM

IN HEMP-WOVEN HAMMOCKS READING THE NATION

This is the season when the husbands lie
in their hemp-woven hammocks for the last time
reading the *Nation* in waning autumn light
before dusk rises from the earth
before the not-knowing if (ever) (again) the earth
will turn on its axis to the light, the great furnace
of the light, will it return the husbands to the light
in their hemp-woven hammocks reading the *Nation*.

EXSANGUINATION

Life as it unspools
ever more eludes
examination.

We wonder what is best—
exsanguination in a rush,
or in 1,000 small slashes.

LITTLE ALBERT, 1920

I was Little Albert.
Nine months old in the famous film.
In a white cotton nightie, on a lab
table sitting upright
facing a camera.
Remember me? Sure.
You do.

First, you saw that I was a "curious" baby.
You saw that I blinked and stared
with all the intensity of an infant-brain
eager to suck into its galaxy of neurons
all of the world. You saw that
I was *you*.

You saw that I was a "fearless" baby.
You saw that I was not frightened
of a burning newspaper held before me
at an alarmingly close range.
Though indeed my rapt infant-face
expressed the classic *wariness* of our race.

Next, you saw that I was not frightened
of a frisky monkey darting close about me
on a leash. You saw

that I was not frightened
by a large dog brought close to me
nor by a quivering rabbit, nor
a small white rat—
nor even a Santa Claus mask
worn by a menacing male figure
clad in white, shoved close
to my infant face.

You saw that I was attracted to the small white rat.
You saw that I reached out to touch the small white rat.
And as I reached for the small white rat
behind my head came an explosion of noise—
the shock of it sent me sprawling, cringing,
face contorted in terror, mouth
a perfect O of anguish, howling—
as the experimenter John Watson struck
a metal pipe with a hammer.
What a shock!—how terror
rushed through me. How
desperately I crawled
to escape almost toppling
off the edge of the table—
except adult hands restrained me.
Children naturally fear loud noises.
Children naturally fear surprises.
Children naturally fear the unknown.
Children can be taught to fear the known.

The second experiment was one month later.
No escape for me for I was Little Albert.

Grim as a little gargoyle
in white cotton nightie able
to sit upright though now wary,
distrustful. No joy in my little body
as (again) a small white rat
was introduced to me. You saw
how this time I shrank away. How
this time there was terror in my face.
How this time I did not reach
with infant eagerness for the small white rat
for I'd learned to fear and hate
the small white rat. And again
(you saw) how the very presence
of the small white rat
precipitated a deafening clamor
as John Watson another time
struck a metal pipe
with a hammer again, again and
again behind my head for
who was there
to stop him? In this way
establishing on film
how (baseless) fear can be instilled
in a subject where fear had
not previously existed and
how memory of this (baseless) fear
will endure contained
in the unfathomable brain.

How I cried and cried! As if
I'd known that my mother had

received but one dollar for
the use of me in John Watson's psych lab
in the experiment that would destroy me
and make John Watson famous.
For in the alchemy of my brain
my fear of a small white rat
had become *generalized*
and now (as Watson ably demonstrated)
I feared the monkey, the dog, the rabbit
equally though each was unaccompanied
by a clanging hammer.
Now I feared the menacing figure
in the Santa Claus mask as if
understanding that Santa Claus
was my tormentor. Cried
and cried and could not be
consoled, even a woman's
fur coat terrified me for
how could I trust *softness*?
Sudden movements, sounds
behind my head—
the unexpected . . .

Classic Pavlovian conditioning.
Bedrock of behavioral psychology.
Brilliant pioneer John Watson!

You are wondering: did John Watson
de-condition me? No. He did not.
Did another experimental psychologist
de-condition me? No. He did not.

Ask me what was the remainder of my life.
Ask me did I adjust to life after the
infamous experiment. Ask me
did I overcome my terror of animals?—
the answer is not known for
I died of hydrocephalus at age six.

All this was long ago. Things are different now.
John Watson would not be allowed to terrorize
Little Albert in his famous experiment now.
Ours is an *ethical* age.

Or was it all a bad dream? Were you deceived?
You were Little Albert? You were conditioned
to fear and hate? You were conditioned to
thrust from you what you were meant to love?
You were the victim? You were the experimental subject?
You were Little Albert, who died young?

HARLOW'S MONKEYS

> Assume that we are not monsters for
> we mean well.
> —*Harry Harlow (1905–1981)*

1.

To be a Monkey
is to be funny

If funny
you don't hurt

& if you don't hurt
you don't cry

& if you don't cry
the noise you make is funny

& if it is funny
people can laugh

for it is *all right*
for people to laugh
at a Monkey

& people are happy
if people laugh

& the one thing they agree
is a Monkey is funny

2.

Oh! it is *not funny*
to hear a Monkey
scream for a Monkey
scream is identical
to a human scream
& a human scream is
not funny

So in the Monkey Lab
to maintain calm
Dr. Harlow had
no choice but
to "surgically remove"
Monkey vocal cords

so if there is a (Monkey) scream
not heard
how is it a *scream?*

3.

We were Harlow's Monkeys
& Dr. Harlow was our Daddy
in the famous lab
at Madison, Wisconsin
from which you did not leave
alive

hairless bawling infants
taken from our mothers
at birth to dwell
in Harlow's hell

"social isolation"
"maternal deprivation"

to be a Monkey
is funny
nursing the dugs
of a bare-wire doll

clinging to
a towel
draped over
a bare-wire doll

seeking milk, love
where there's none
yet: seeking milk,
love where

there's none.
yet: seeking

How could a Monkey
be sad, could a Monkey
spell the word—"sad"—?

In the bottom
of the Monkey cage
listless & broken
  when the wire doll too
  is taken away

"learned helplessness"
"pit of despair"

You laugh, for you
would never so despair
mistaking a wire doll
for a Mother
or a devil
for a Daddy

4.

(Look: in any lab
you had
to be cruel
to publish

& succeed.
As Israel, Harry
changed his name
to Harlow, Harry
to publish
& succeed.

Just had
to be cruel
the way today
a baby calf
in its cage
grows
slowly
to veal.)

OBEDIENCE: 1962

1.

Because it was explained to you, you must follow orders.
Because the white coat explained to you, you must follow orders.
Because the voice of the white coat explained to you, you must
follow orders.
Because *the white male voice* explained to you, you must follow
orders.

> Because the laboratory setting explained to you, you must follow
> orders.
> Because the fluorescent lights explained to you, you must follow
> orders.
> Because the turreted university explained to you, you must
> follow orders.

2.

Because it was 1962, in the wake of the trial of Adolf Eichmann.
Because the question was—*How could human beings perpetrate such
acts upon one another?*
Because to understand the Holocaust you must understand
the soul of humankind.

Not what the soul speaks but how the soul behaves you must understand.

Because you agreed to participate in an experiment testing "memory" in the laboratory of Stanley Milgram at Yale.

Because you agreed to participate in an experiment testing the relationship of punishment to "memory."

Because the experiment in "memory" was not an experiment in "memory" but in "obedience"—(it was not explained to you).

Because Stanley Milgram wanted to understand the Holocaust.

Because Stanley Milgram would have perished in the Holocaust if he'd been born in Europe like his Jewish relatives, so Stanley Milgram wanted to understand the Holocaust in the only way a scientist can understand which is through experimentation.

Through an experiment enacted upon a subject kept in ignorance of the perimeter of the experiment.

Through an experiment enacted upon a subject kept in ignorance that he was in fact the subject.

Because it was explained to you, you would play the role of the "teacher" in the experiment.

Because it was explained to you, the "teacher" must follow the orders given him.

Because it was explained to you, the "teacher" must punish the "learner" when he errs.

Because it was explained to you, if there is punishment there must be one who is punished.

Because it was explained to you, if there is punishment there must be a punisher.

Because the learner was in another room, you could not see his face when you administered shocks to him.

(True, you could hear the learner's screams. But you could not see his face.)

(If you cannot see the face, is there a victim?)
(If you do not know the name, is there a victim?)
(If you are not to be blamed, can you be blamed?)
Because the voltage was mild at first—fifteen volts.
Because the voltage rose slowly—forty volts, seventy volts . . .
Because *eager to please.*
Because *good.*
Because *obey.*
Because four dollars an hour.
. . . two hundred twenty volts, three hundred volts . . .
Because it was explained to you, you must continue to the end.
Because it was explained to you, *you would not be blamed.*
Because you broke into a sweat of anguish and yet—you obeyed.
Because you broke into hysterical laughter and yet—you obeyed.
Must follow orders, continue to the end, will not be blamed—you obeyed.
. . . four hundred seventy-five volts.

3.

Because in the deep brain, the chanting of elders.
Do as we say. Do as we say. Do as we say.
Because in the deep brain, the elders have no pity.
Do as we say. Do as we say. Do as we say.
Because in the deep brain, no soul but pebbles thrust into the
mouth.
Do as we say. Do as we say. Do as we say.
Because the Holocaust was not possible without following orders.
Because the Holocaust was not possible without continuing to the
end.
Because the Holocaust was not possible without *you.*

Fifty years live and relive the infamous experiment through the ruin of your life.

Fifty years sleepless made to recall the silence after you'd delivered four hundred seventy-five volts . . .

Fifty years shame, you'd killed a human being.

Followed orders, to the end. Nor would being debriefed lessen the horror—*Killed a human being.*

For it was explained to you at last, the protocol of the experiment. The role you'd played, you had not realized.

The acts you'd perpetrated, you had not realized.

No volts, no shocks. No "learner."

Only you, the "teacher." Yet not a "teacher."

You, the experimental subject.

Always and only *you.*

Everyone in the lab was in collusion against *you.*

All of history was in collusion against *you.*

Not your fault. Following orders. Continue to the end.

You will not be blamed.

LONEY

Old fears in dead of night
like lozenges
stuck dry
on the tongue.
Wakened numb
as Novocain.

In dead of night ask
For God's sake what
did you miss. You know
God-damned well you
have missed what
they hid from you.

The lost, the loney.
You knew them too late.
Dying too soon.
The young uncle you'd loved most.
Killed himself to free
his spirit, trapped like a genie
in a Coke bottle.

Never knew why. How
was a secret too whispered
in the cornstalks.

Misshapen ears of corn,
wizened faces. By November
you could see them
seeing you along the rows
of stalks.

You ran from the faces,
hid your eyes. Gut-kick,
spine-cold, sick
with fear of what
had no name.

Oh that was terrible! Just—
terrible . . . Something
like that, in a family—
you never forget.

Forty years ago.
Like yesterday.

A rifle, he'd used. You knew
this—didn't you? One of his.
Somehow he'd missed where
he was aiming. Not once,
not twice, three times pulled
the trigger pressing the barrel
against his chest . . .

We heard the shots
at the back of the house
and then the quiet.

It's the quiet
after gunshots you remember.

THE COMING STORM

Oblivion was a familiar blue sky, once.
And the lake, too, familiar though now turned to ink.

That border of marshgrass luridly bright!
Sun-glaring amid darkness as a demon eye.

If it's 1859 you believe, probably,
in the radiant soul. That single white sail
at the prow of oblivion.
Or are you, a man in shirtsleeves, that solitary rower
in an invisible boat? Straining at the oars
and never to reach shore.
As by quickened pulsebeat the end-of-things
blows out of the fabled Northeast.

Oh, oblivion! That gnarly tarry taste.
That smell of airborne wet.
You won't have time even for prayer.

Or have you become a paper cutout in red shirt,
Beige vest, straw hat, a figure jauntily seated
at the edge of the nightmare lake?
A fisherman? That's what you are?

And your little dog?
At the edge of the pit?
Oh, where are the adults who once loved you,
and stood guard?

(Martin Johnson Heade, *The Coming Storm*, 1859)

EDWARD HOPPER'S "ELEVEN A.M.," 1926

She's naked yet wearing shoes.
Wants to think *nude*. And happy in her body.

Though it's a fleshy aging body. And her posture
in the chair—leaning forward, arms on knees,
staring out the window—makes her belly bulge,
but what the hell.

What the hell, *he* isn't here.

Lived in this damn drab apartment at Third Avenue,
Twenty-third Street, Manhattan, how many
damn years, has to be at least fifteen. Moved to the city
from Hackensack needing to breathe.

She'd never looked back. Sure they called her selfish,
cruel. What the hell, the use they'd have made of her,
she'd be sucked dry like bone marrow.

First job was file clerk at Trinity Trust. Wasted
three years of her young life waiting
for R.B. to leave his wife and wouldn't you think
a smart girl like her would know better?

Second job also file clerk but then she'd been promoted
to Mr. Castle's secretarial staff at Lyman Typewriters. The
least the old bastard could do for her and she'd
have done a lot better except for fat-face Stella Czechi.

Third job, Tvek Realtors & Insurance and she's
Mr. Tvek's private secretary—*What would I do
without you my dear one?*

As long as Tvek pays her decent. And *he* doesn't
let her down like last Christmas, she'd wanted to die.

This damn room she hates. Dimlit like a region of the soul
into which light doesn't penetrate. Soft-shabby old furniture
and sagging mattress like those bodies in dreams we feel
but don't see. But she keeps her bed made
every God-damn day visitors or not.

He doesn't like disorder. *He'd* told her how he'd learned
to make a proper bed in the U.S. Army in 1917.

The trick is, *he* says, you make the bed as soon as you get up.

Detaches himself from her as soon as it's over. Sticky skin,
hairy legs, patches of scratchy hair on his shoulders, chest,
belly. She'd like him to hold her and they could drift into
sleep together but rarely this happens. She hates feeling the
nerves twitching in his legs. He'd leap from her as soon as he
came she thinks, the bastard.

Crazy wanting her, then abruptly it's over—*he*'s inside his head,
and *she's* inside hers.

Now this morning she's thinking God-damn bastard, this has
got to be the last time. Waiting for him to call to explain
the night before when he didn't show up. She'd
waited from 8 P.M. until midnight and in those hours
sick with hating him and hating herself and yet—the leap
of hope when the phone rang. Telling her
Unavoidable, crisis at home. Love you.

Now she's waiting for him to call again. And there's the chance
he might come here before calling which he has done more than
once. *Couldn't keep away.*
God, I'm crazy for you.

In this somber painting by Edward Hopper who could paint only
his wife since Jo Hopper was jealous of nude models you can't see
her face but it's a girl's face grown heavy and pouty, and her lips
lipstick-red, sulky-brunette face still damned good-looking and *he*
knows it, he's excited seeing men on the street following her with
their eyes then it turns sour and he blames *her.*

She's thinking she will give the bastard ten more minutes.

She's Jo Hopper with her plain red-head's face stretched
on this fleshy female's face and *he's* the artist but also
the lover and last week he'd come to take her
out to Delmonico's but in this dimlit room they'd made love
in her bed and never got out until too late and she'd overheard
him on the phone *explaining*—there's the sound of a man's voice
explaining to a wife that is so callow, so craven, she's sick
with contempt recalling. Yet *he* says he has left his family, he loves *her.*

Runs his hands over her body like a blind man trying to see. And
the radiance in his face that's pitted and scarred, he needs her in the
way a starving man needs food. *Die without you. Don't
leave me.*

Once in secret she'd seen him in the street with his younger son,
scrawny boy of thirteen, father and son walking together so bonded
they didn't need to talk. Sharing a mood of solitude like
their hawk-faces and widow's-peak black hair. The son
will grow into the father she saw and felt a stab of humiliation,
excluded.

He'd told her it wasn't what she thought. Wasn't his family
that kept him from loving her all he could but his life
he'd never told anyone about in the war, in the infantry,
in France. What crept like paralysis through him.
Things that had happened to him, and things
that he'd witnessed, and things that he'd perpetrated himself
with his own hands. And she'd taken his hands and kissed
them, and brought them against her breasts that were aching
like the breasts of a young mother ravenous to give suck,
and sustenance. And she said *No. That is your old life.*
I am your new life.

She will give her new life five more minutes.

II.

———

THE FIRST ROOM

THE FIRST ROOM

In every dream of a room
the first room intrudes.
No matter the years, the tears dried
and forgotten, it is the skeleton
of the first that protrudes.

SINKHOLES

take you where
you don't want to go.

Where you'd been
and had passed smilingly through,
and were alive. Then.

THAT OTHER

They laughed, but no. You
don't remember that.

What you think you remember—
it wasn't *that*.

Yes—you remember
some things. And
some things did
happen. Except not
that way.

And anyway, not
to *you*.

THE MERCY

So much depends
upon
forgetting much

for our
earliest
yearnings never
abandon us.

The stroke
that wipes out
memory
is another word
for mercy.

THE BLESSING

Barefoot daring
to walk
amid
the thrashing eye-glitter
of what remains
when the tide
retreats
we ask ourselves
why did it matter
so much
to have the last
word?
or any
word?

Here, please—
take what
remains.
It is yours.

THIS IS NOT A POEM

in which the poet discovers
delicate white-parched bones
of a small creature
on a Great Lake shore
    or the desiccated remains
    of cruder road-kill
beside the rushing highway.

Nor is it a poem in which
a cracked mirror yields
a startled face,
or sere grasses hiss-
ing like consonants
in a foreign language.
Family photo album
filled with yearning
strangers long-deceased,
closet of beautiful
clothes of the dead.
Attic trunk, stone well
or metonymic moon
time-traveling for wisdom
in the Paleolithic
age, in the Middle Kingdom
or Genesis
or the time of Basho . . . .

Instead it is a slew
of words in search
of a container—
a sleek green stalk,
a transparent lung,
a single hair's curl,
a cooing of vowels
like doves.

APOCALYPSO

Something thrill-
ing in cata-
clysm &
in the col-
lapse of Empires.

Irrevocable, ir-
remediable,
Apocalypso
& this myriad
bloom-
ing buzz
in which,
we'd hoped,
we might
have steered
more bravely,
sensibly &
to more pur-
pose, the
effort of be-
ing human,
& "moral"
& "good"
coming,

at last,
finally
terribly
& simply
to
The End

III.

AMERICAN MELANCHOLY

TO MARLON BRANDO IN HELL

Because you suffocated your beauty in fat.
Because you made of our adoration, mockery.
Because you were the predator male, without remorse.

Because you were the greatest of our actors, and you threw away
greatness like trash.
Because you could not take seriously what others took as their lives.
Because in this you made mockery of our lives.

Because you died encased in fat
And even then, you'd lived too long.

Because you loathed yourself, and made of yourself a loathsome
person.
Because the wheelchair paraplegic of *The Men* was made to suffocate
in the fat of the bloated Kurtz.
Because your love was carelessly sown, debris tossed from a
speeding vehicle.
And because you loved both men and women, except not enough.

Because the slow suicide of self-disgust is horrible to us, and fascinating
as the collapse of tragedy into farce is fascinating
and the monstrousness of festered beauty.

Because you lured a girl of 15 to deceive her parents on a wintry-dark December school day, 1953.

Because you lured this girl to lie about where she was going, what she was doing, in the most reckless act of her young life.

Because you lured this girl to take a Greyhound bus from Williamsville, New York, to downtown Buffalo, New York, alone in the wintry dusk, as she had not ever been *alone* in her previous life.

Because you lured this girl, shivering, daring to step onto the bus in front of Williamsville High School at 4:55 P.M. to be taken twelve miles to the small shabby second-run Main Street Cinema for a 6:00 P.M. showing of *The Wild One*—a place that would've been forbidden, if the girl's parents had known.

What might have happened!—by chance, did not happen.

Because inside the Main Street Cinema were rows of seats near-empty in the dark, commingled smells of stale popcorn and cigarette smoke—(for this was an era when there was "smoking in the loge"), and on the screen the astonishing magnified figure of "Johnny" in black leather jacket, opaque dark sunglasses, on his motorcycle exuding the sulky authority of the young predator-male.

Because when asked what you were rebelling against, you said with wonderful disdain, *What've you got?*

Because that was our answer too, that we had not such words to utter.

Because as Johnny you took us on the outlaw motorcycle, we clung to your waist like the sleep of children.

Because as Johnny you were the face of danger, and you were unrepentant.

Because as Johnny you could not say *Thank you.*

Because as Johnny you abandoned us in the end.

Because on that motorcycle you grew smaller and smaller on the road out of the small town, and vanishing.

Because you have vanished. Because in plain sight you vanished.

Because the recklessness of adolescence is such elation, the heart is filled to bursting.

Because recklessness is the happy quotient of desperation, and contiguous with shame, and yet it is neither of these, and greater than the sum of these.

Because the girl will recall through her life how you entered her life like sunlight illuminating a landscape wrongly believed to be denuded of beauty.

Because there is a savage delight in loss, and in the finality of loss.

Because at age twenty-three on Broadway you derailed *A Streetcar Named Desire*, and made the tragedy of Blanche DuBois the first of your triumphs.

So defiantly Stanley Kowalski, there has been none since.

Because after Brando, all who follow are failed impersonators.

Bawling and bestial and funny, crude laughter of the Polack male, the humiliation of the Southern female whose rape is but another joke.

Because you were the consummate rapist, with the swagger of the rapist enacting the worst brute will of the audience.

Because you were Terry Malloy, the screen filled with your battered boy's face.

Because sweetness and hurt were conjoined in that face.

Because you took up the glove dropped by Eva Marie Saint, and put it on your hand, appropriating the blond Catholic girl and wearing her like a glove.

Because you exposed your soul in yearning—*I could've been a contender!*—knowing how defeat, failure, ignominy would be your fate.

Because in 1955 at the age of thirty-one, after having won an Academy Award for *On the Waterfront*, you were interviewed by Edward R. Murrow wreathed in cigarette smoke like a shroud and in your rented stucco house in the hills above Los Angeles already you were speaking of trying to be "normal." Because you endured the interviewer's lame questions—"Have you discovered that success can have its own problems?"—"Are you planning a long career as an actor?"
Because you conceded, "I can't do anything else well."
Because you said you wanted to sing and dance on screen, you wanted to be "superficial"—you wanted to "entertain."
Because on the mantel of the rented house was a portrait of your mother at forty, your alcoholic mother who'd failed to love you enough.

Because your discomfort with the interview was evident.
Because you spoke of the fear of losing "anonymity" when already "anonymity" was lost.
Because the awkwardly staged interview ended with you playing bongo drums with another drummer, in the bizarrely decorated basement of the rented house. Because quickly then your hands slapped the drums with a kind of manic precision, your eyes half-shut, a goofy happiness softened your face.

Because at this moment it was not (yet) too late.

Because you grew into the predator male careless in fatherhood fathering eleven children whom you would scarcely know and of whom three were with your Guatemalan housekeeper.
Because you were the absent father of a drug-addled son most like yourself except lacking your talent ("Christian") who shot to death the fiancé of his younger sister ("Cheyenne") in your house in Los Angeles, was incarcerated for manslaughter, and died young; and the absent father of the "Cheyenne" who hanged herself soon after the murder, aged twenty-five.

Because your beauty seduced you, and made of you a prankster.
Because the prankster always goes too far, that is the essence of *prank*.
Because you were a prankster, sowing death like semen.
Because all you had, you had to squander.

Because you tried, like Paul Muni, to disappear into film.
Because you were Mark Antony, Sky Masterson, Zapata, Fletcher Christian, Napoleon! You were the clownish cross-dresser-outlaw of *One-Eyed Jacks*—a film debacle you'd directed yourself. You were Vito Corleone and you were the garrulous bald fat Kurtz of *Apocalypse Now*, mumbling and staggering in the dark, bloated American madness.

Because as the widower Paul of *Last Tango in Paris* you stripped your sick soul bare, in the radiance of disintegration. Because you were stunned in terror of annihilation yet played the clown, baring your buttocks on a Parisian dance floor.

Because confounded by the corpse of the dead beautiful wife framed ludicrously in flowers you could hardly speak, and then you spoke too much. Because you were stupid in grief. Because you could not forgive.

Wipe off the cosmetic mask! You hadn't known the dead woman, and you would not know the dead woman, who had not been faithful to you. All you can know is the compliant body of your lover far too young for you, and only as a body.

The futility of male sexuality, as a bulwark against death.

The farce of male sexuality, as a bulwark against death.

Because nonetheless you danced with astonishing drunken grace, with the girl young as a daughter. On the tango dance floor you spun, you fell to your knees, you shrugged off your coat, you were wearing a proper shirt and a tie to belie drunkenness and despair, fell flat on your back on the dance floor amid oblivious dancers and yet at once in rebuke of all expectation you were on your feet again and—dancing . . .

And in a drunken parody of tango you were unexpectedly light on your feet, radiant in playfulness, clowning, in mockery of the heightened emotions and sexual drama of tango—as in your youth you'd wanted to be "superficial" and to "entertain"—

And then, lowering your trousers and baring your buttocks in the exhilaration of contempt.

Because the actor does not exist, if he is not the center of attention.

Because the actor's heart is an emptiness, no amount of adulation can fill.

Because after the slapstick-tango you lay curled in the exhaustion of grief and in the muteness of grief, a fetal corpse on a balcony in gray-lit Paris.

In Hell, there is *tango*. The other dancers dance on.

Because you made of self-loathing a caprice of art.
Because what was good in you, your social conscience, your generosity to liberal causes, was swallowed up in the *other*.
Because you squandered yourself in a sequence of stupid films as if in defiance of your talent and of our expectations of that talent.
Because by late middle age you'd lived too long.

Where there has been such love,
there can be no forgiveness

Because at eighty you'd endured successive stages of yourself, like a great tree suffocated in its own rings, beginning to rot from within.
Because when you died, we understood that you had died long before.
Because we could not forgive you, who had thrown greatness away.

Because you have left us. And we are lonely.
And we would join you in Hell, if you would have us.

TOO YOUNG TO MARRY BUT NOT TOO YOUNG TO DIE

Drowned together in his car in Lake Chippewa.
It was a bright cold starry night on Lake Chippewa.
Lake Chippewa was a "living" lake then
though soon afterward it would choke and die.

In the bright cold morning after we could spy
them only through a patch of ice brushed clear of snow.
Scarcely three feet below,
they were oblivious to us.

Together beneath the ice in each other's arms.
Jean-Marie's head rested on Troy's shoulder.
Their hair had floated up and was frozen.
Their eyes were open in the perfect lucidity of death.

Calmly they sat upright. Not a breath!
It was 1967, there were no seat belts
to keep them apart. Beautiful
as mannequins in Slater Brothers' window.
Faces flawless, not a blemish.
Yet—you could believe
they might be breath-
ing, for some trick

of scintillate light revealed
tiny bubbles in the ice,
and a motion like a smile
in Jean-Marie's perfect face.

How far Troy'd driven the car onto Lake Chippewa
before the ice creaked, and cracked, and opened
like the parting of giant jaws—at least fifty feet!
This was a feat like Troy's 7-foot-3.8-inch high jump.

In the briny snow you could see the car tracks
along the shore where in summer sand
we'd sprawl and soak up sun
in defiance of skin carcinomas-to-come. And you could see
how deftly he'd turned the wheel onto the ice
at just the right place.
And on the ice you could see
how he'd made the tires spin and grab
and Jean-Marie clutching his hand *Oh oh oh!*

The sinking would be silent, and slow.

Eastern edge of Lake Chippewa, shallower
than most of the lake but deep enough at twelve feet
to suck down Mr. Dupuy's Chevy
so all that was visible from shore
was the gaping ice wound.
And then in the starry night
a drop to −5 degrees Fahrenheit
and ice freezing over the sunken car.
Who would have guessed it, of Lake Chippewa!

Now in the morning through the swept ice
there's a shocking intimacy just below.
With our mittens we brush away powder snow.
With our boots we kick away ice chunks.
Lie flat and stare through the ice
Seeing Jean-Marie Schuter and Troy Dupuy
as we'd never seen them in life.
Our breaths steam in Sunday-morning light.

It will be something we must live with—
the couple do not care about our astonishment.
Perfect in love, and needing no one to applaud
as they'd been oblivious to our applause
at the Herkimer Junior High prom where they were
crowned Queen and King three years before.
(In Herkimer County, New York, you grew up fast.
The body matured, the brain lagged behind
like the slowest runner on the track team
we'd applaud with affection mistaken for teen mockery.)

No one wanted to summon help just yet.
It was a dreamy silence above ice as below.
And the ice a shifting hue—silvery, ghost-gray, pale
blue—as the sky shifts overhead
like a frowning parent. *What!*
Lake Chippewa was where some of us went ice-fishing
with our grandfathers. Sometimes, we skated.
Summers there were speedboats, canoes. There'd been
drownings in Lake Chippewa we'd heard
but no one of *ours*.

Police, firetruck, ambulance sirens would rend the air.
Strangers would shout at one another.
We'd be ordered back—off the ice of Lake Chippewa
that shone with beauty and onto the littered shore.
By harsh daylight made to see
Mr. Dupuy's 1963 Chevy
hooked like a great doomed fish.
All that privacy yanked upward pitiless
and streaming icy rivulets!
We knew it was wrong to disturb the frozen lovers
and make of them mere bodies.

Sweet-lethal embrace of Lake Chippewa
But no embrace can survive thawing.

One of us, Gordy Garrison, would write a song,
"Too Young to Marry but Not Too Young to Die"
(echo of Bill Monroe's "I Saw Her Little Footprints
in the Snow"), which he'd sing with his band the Raiders,
accompanying himself on the Little Martin guitar
he'd bought from his cousin Art Garrison
when Art enlisted in the U.S. Navy and for a while
it was all you'd hear at Herkimer High, where the Raiders
played for Friday-night dances in the gym, but then
we graduated and things changed and nothing
more came of Gordy's song or of the Raiders.

"TOO YOUNG TO MARRY BUT NOT TOO YOUNG TO DIE"
was the headline in the *Herkimer Packet*.
We scissored out the front-page article, kept it for decades in a
bedroom drawer.

(No one ever moves in Herkimer except
those who move away, and never come back.)
The clipping is yellowed, deeply creased,
and beginning to tear. When some of us stare
at the photos our hearts cease beating—oh, just a beat!

It was something we'd learned to live with—
there'd been no boy desperate to die with any of us.
We'd have accepted, probably—*yes*.
Deep breath, shuttered eyes—*yes, Troy*.
Secret kept yellowed and creased in the drawer
though if you ask, laughingly we'd deny it.

We see Gordy sometimes, and his wife, June. Our grand-
children are friends. Hum Gordy's old song
to make Gordy blush a fierce apricot hue
but it seems cruel, we're all on blood
thinners now.

DOCTOR HELP ME

Because no one can know.
Because they would hate me forever.
Because they would never forgive me for shaming them.
Because they would kill me.

Because it was my first time, what he made me do.
Because it was only that once. Because it is not fair!
Because I am afraid of how it will hurt to have a baby, I am so
afraid.

Because they will know at school. They will send me home.
Because my grandma is very sick, it will be a shameful shock
to her.

Because I am too old. I have had my babies, I have had five babies
that lived. If there is another now I think I will die.

Because I told my husband, it was a risk. Because he did not listen.

Because I hate him. Because I am so tired.

Because I am not well . . .

Because I am out of breath and there is a pain in my chest, sometimes I think that I will faint.

On the stairs at work I will faint, I will fall and everyone will know.

Because if they lift me, and my shirt is lifted, they will see the belly, and the waist of the jeans that no longer snaps shut.

Because my husband will know it was not him.

Because that will be the end of our family.

Because I will have to kill myself before that.

Because there is diabetes in our family, I am afraid to have a blood test.

Because I have never been to any hospital. No one in our family has.

Because we do not believe in blood transplants—(is that what it is called?)—the Bible forbids.

Because the father is gone. Because he is not coming back.
Because the father would kill me, if he knew.
Because the father is married.
Because the father has too many children already!
Because the father would deny it, he would say that I am lying.
Because the father would say that it was my fault, that I did not stop him.
Because he has called me *bitch, slut* when he was angry, when there was no reason.
Because he would never love me again.

Because I am too young, doctor! Because I want to finish school.
Because I don't know how this happened. I did not want it to happen.
Because it is the same man as with my sister.
Because he is engaged to my sister. Because my sister cannot know!
Because it is a secret, he said he would strangle me if I told.

Because I will lose my job. Because I can't keep lifting heavy sacks, if they find out they will fire me.
Because I won't be able to commute ninety minutes a day.
Because I can't afford to lose my job, I will be evicted.
Because I have three children already, they would be shamed.

Because he is so old!

Because he is too young, he is immature and shiftless.

Because he went away into the Army. Because he could not come home out of shame.

Because he is my best friend's father.

Because he lives next door. Because we would see him all the time and his family would see the baby.

Because they would not believe me if I told his name.

Because he is a "man of God," they would believe him, anything he said.

Because he has made me promise, no one can know.

Because it was not my fault!

Because I did not want to be with him in that way but he made me to prove that I loved him. Because if there is a baby he will never love me again.

Because we might become engaged. If this goes away.

Because nobody will love me again and I would not blame them.

Because everyone who knows will speak of me in scorn and disgust. Because they will say of me, she has broken her parents' heart, she is a

whore.

Because I tried to do it to myself, with an icepick. But I was too afraid, I could not.

Because I hit myself with my fists in the stomach. Because I was sick to my stomach, vomiting and choking, but it did not help.

Because there is no hope for me, doctor. If you do not help me. Because God will understand. It is just this one time.

OLD AMERICA HAS COME HOME TO DIE

Old America has come home to die.
From Oklahoma oil fields where the sun
beat his head and brains boiling in a stew
of old memories. *Penance for my sins*
I never owned up to.

From Juneau, Alaska, where he'd fished
coho salmon on the *Mary Flynn*.
From Black Fly, Ontario,
where he'd been a hobo farmhand,
and from New Jericho, Manitoba,
where he'd mined gypsum sand,
Old America has come home to die.
Bad memories like shreds of tobacco on the tongue,
you can't spit off.

From Big Sky, Montana, where
he'd been a cowboy. From
Western Pacific, Sandusky,
and Santa Fe Railway, from the Gulf
Islands and Skagit River, Washington,
where he'd worked construction,
Old America has come home to die.
Bosses treat you like shit on their shoe
they can scrape off any time.

And they do.

From the Great Lakes, where
he'd worked freighters
in minus-
zero
weather, lost
half his damn fingers and toes
to frostbite. From the mines
at Crater Falls, Idaho, where
his lungs turned the hue
of anthracite. And from Moab,
Utah, where he'd been incarcerated
seven years for a rob-
bery he hadn't done,
Old America has come home to die.
Romantic life of a "hobo"
lasts until your legs go.

Old America freckled with melanomas,
straggly hair to his shoulders
like the boy-General Custer, and
fester-
ing sores
on his back, sides, and belly
has come home to die
where no one remembers him—
"Uncle Eli?"
who'd sent postcards
from the West long faded
in Granma's photo album

as out of a void
in an era before Polaroid
Old America has come home to die.
Old America with a blind left eye.
Old America with a stump
of his gangrenous left leg, amp-
utated at the knee.
How bad I treated my family
who loved me.
Come home to say I am sorry and I love you.

Great-Granma's youngest sister's
son Eli who'd left the farm in 1931
to work on the Erie Canal, but no—
disappeared somewhere west
beyond Pocatello, Idaho. We'd guessed
you'd died in the Yukon, or in
the Eagle Mine in Utah. Capsized
in the Bering Strait, or vaporized
at the Fearing Nevada Test Site
or murdered by railroad cops
and flung into the Mississippi—
poor Uncle Eli!

Sins I have committed these many
years, I regret. Wash my soul
clean before I die.
Trying to explain why
he'd left home except—
Where is Marta? Please

let me see Marta—his brother's wife
he was in love with, and Marta told him
she was pregnant, and he abandoned
her to her violent husband like a coward.
Years I never thought of Marta, or Ma—
any of you. Now, that's all I think about.
Forgive me how bad I behaved
when I was young . . .

Old America, we are not cruel
people, but the fact is mostly we've
forgotten you. And Great-Aunt Marta
too—died in 1961. And her oldest
son Ethan, who'd be the one
you'd want to see, is gone, too—
somewhere south of the 38th parallel,
Korea.
Where are my brothers—Frank, Joseph, Frederic?
My sisters—Margaret, Elizabeth?
My cousin Leah?—so many cousins . . .
Old America, frantic to repent,
has brought us presents—
flute carved out of a walrus tusk, Inuit
doll and soapstone skulls, beaded belts and
miniature pelts and something that causes Maya to scream,
Oh God—is that an Indian scalp?

Old America has come home to die
this first week of December
in time for Maya to videotape

an interview with Great-Uncle Eli
for her American Studies seminar at Wesleyan—
Life of an Oldtime "Hobo."
Her classmates will be impressed—
Old America is like awesome, fantastic—
and her professor will grade an A—
Tragic, vividly rendered & iconic.

JUBILATE:

An Homage in Catterel* Verse

For I will consider my Cat Cherie
for she is the very apotheosis of Cat-Beauty
which is to say, nothing extraordinary
for in the Cat, beauty *is* ordinary
like the bliss
conferred
upon us
in the hypnosis
of purr-
ing.
She has been known
to knead her claws
upon a sleeve.
And on a knee.
And on bare skin,
sharp claws sinking in—
just a warning.
For she is of the *tribe of Tyger*
and eyes *burning bright*
though cuddling
at night

---

* "Catterel"—an elevated variant of "doggerel."

until you wake to discover—
where is she? *Cher-ie?*
Don't inquire.

For in considering my Cat Cherie
I am considering Catitude—
each Cat the (essential)
equivalent of all others
not varying freak-

ishly in size
(like crude D*gs)
but pleas-
ingly Platonic.
Cat-chutzpah
is the "sheathed
claw"—
no heart borne
upon a foreleg,
but
your challenge
to decode,
like poetry
of a subtlety
that *does not bark*
its meaning
but forces us to
be just a little

smarter than
we are.
(Unlike D*gs
whose un-
critical adulation
makes us
dumber.)

Of Twitter it is estimated
somewhere beyond thirty-one percent
who tweet are feline,
in nocturnal prowl
slyly retweeting
their kind,
reproducing,
replicating
the dark rapacious ever-
fecund *feral soul*
that is the sea
upon which "civilization"
floats, uneasily.
For such eloquent Kitty-Twitter,
only the most elegant Kitty-Litter.
But if you ask, *Cherie, what
is this?*, the reply is
blank blinking innocence.
Mew? What's with you?

❀ ❀ ❀

—"Live free
or die"—is the Cat's
very soul, that
makes of us,
by contrast,
fawning and obsequious
beings (not unlike
D*gs). Such beauty
instructs us in its own
perfection
for it is beyond
mere "use"—no *work-
cats, watch-cats,
plebian beings*
but each descended
of gods
as ancient Egypt
honored; and how
like a deity, to sink
teeth into a rat,
a creature that
squeamish
mankind abhors,
while maintaining
purest Cat-
innocence.

Sandpaper tongue,
utter long-
ing.
Cat-love the nudge
of furry-hard head.
But oh, where has she gone?
Kitty-kitty-*kitty*! She may come
when called
(like the D*g)
but mostly
she will not
for
(unlike the D*g),
she has got
an interior life,
inscrutable,
inaccessible,
unpossessable.
She does not aim
to please, or aim
at all. Her blessing
is a fluke, as readily
withdrawn as given.
Never will she *do your bidding*.
Never will she falsely flatter,
nor deceive you
that you much matter
beyond the reach
of the hand that pets
and feeds.

Also she has got
much busyness
out-of-doors
by moonlight.
Don't inquire.

But there she has gone
headfirst through
the Plexiglas cat door
to return with,
dropped on the floor
at my feet,
a small carcass very still.
Oh Cherie, what have you done?

Only the Cat's gift is freely given.
The Dog in subservience as in chains
has no free will, and so—
Oh Cherie—is this for me?

For I will consider my Cat Cherie
whose tail switches irritably

across these keys
when confronted with prose
found wanting.
For it is irrefutable, the Cat
is the harshest critic of prose, cattedly
rejecting what has been doggedly
written.
This will not do, at all.
This is not it. At all
where the D*g drools
delight with very mediocrity,
in complicity.
Sometimes, the furry Cat-
sprawl
obliterates the typescript
utterly
for you dare not move
a limb, a tail—
even (gingerly)
from the laptop—
at risk
of provoking a hiss—
Mew! Whom're you touching, you!

If I dare rise
from this desk
prematurely—
if I dare plead

(human) exhaustion—
vehemently
Cherie will dig in her claws
securing my knees
with the cry *Mew!*
Where d'you think you're going, you!
Thus hours, days & ages
accumulate in pages
and pages into books
and books into oeuvres.
Purrlific the literary
judgment.

The very best books (it is said)
are not *ghost-* but *cat*-written.
Simenon, Colette, John le Carré
not least Hemingway—
Auden, Eliot, Philip K. Dick—
Borges and Burroughs and
Patricia Highsmith—
Jean Cocteau and Henry David Thoreau—
H. P. Lovecraft and Edgar Allan Poe—
("I wish I could write as mysterious as a cat!")—
Twain, Bradbury, Raymond Chandler—
Sartre, Sylvia Plath, and—Daniel Handler?—
not least Samuel Johnson—
("But Hodge shan't be shot; no, no Hodge

shall not be shot")—
rapidly retreating into the mists of Time
where Muse is suffused with Mouse
until the two are merged in mystery—
Cat and collaborator.

KITE POEM

for Billy Collins

Some-
thing there
is in the American
soul that soars with
kites that soar! Some-
thing alive with the roar
of the wind lifting the kite
that soars above rooftops, tree-
tops, and awestruck heads! And yet—
Something there is not in the
American soul to adore the
kite that fails to soar.

The kite whose tail
is tattered in the
TV antenna.
The kite that rises
thrillingly
at dawn
then crashes

vertically
at your feet
in a heap.

AMERICAN SIGN LANGUAGE

At the podium
measured and grave as a metronome
the (white, male) poet with bald-
gleaming head broods in gnom-
ic syllables on the death
of twelve-year-old (black) Tamir Rice
shot in a trice in a park
by a Cleveland police officer
claiming to believe
the boy's plastic pistol
was a "real gun"
like his own eager
to discharge and slay

                    while twelve feet away
                    at the edge
                    of the bright-lit stage
                    the (white, female) interpreter
                    signing for the deaf is stricken
                    with emotion—
                    horror, pity, disbelief—
                    outrage, sorrow—
                    young-woman face contorted
                    and eyes spilling tears

like Tamir Rice's mother
perhaps, or the sister
made to witness
the child's bleeding out
in the Cleveland playground.
We are made to stare
as the interpreter's fingers
pluck the poet's words out of
the air
like bullets, break open stanzas
tight as conches with the deft
ferocity of a cormo-
rant and render gnome-speech
raw as hurt, as harm,
as human terror
wet-eyed and mouth-grimace
where words that can be
uttered
cannot follow.

HOMETOWN WAITING FOR YOU

All these decades we've been waiting here for you. Welcome!
You do look lonely.
No one knows you the way we know you.
And *you* know us.

Did you actually (once) tell yourself—*I am better than this?*
One day actually (once) tell yourself—*I deserve better than this?*

Fact is, *you* couldn't escape us.
And we have been waiting for you. Welcome home!
Boasting how a scholarship bore you away
like a chariot of the gods except
where you are born, your soul remains.

We all die young here.
Not one of us outlived *young* here.
Check out obituaries
in the *Lockport Union Sun & Journal.*
Car crash,
overdose.
Gunshot, fire.
Cancers of breast,
ovaries, lung,
colon. Heart
attack, cirrhosis

of liver.
Assault, battery.
Stroke! And—
did I say over-
dose? Car
crash?

Filling up the cemeteries here.
Plastic trash here.
Unbiodegradable Styrofoam here.
Three-quarters of your seventh-
grade class now
in urns, ash.

Those flashy cars
you'd have given your soul
to ride in,
just once, now
eyeless
rusting hulks
in tall grass.
Those eyes you'd
wished might crawl
upon you like ants,
in graveyards
of broken glass.

Atwater Park where
you'd wept
in obscure shame
and now whatever

his name who'd trampled
your heart, he's
ash.

Proud as hell
of you though
(we admit)
never read a
goddamn word
you've written.

We never forgave you. We hate winners.

Still, it's not too late.
Did I say overdose?
Why otherwise are you here?

IV.

"*THIS IS THE TIME . . .*"

HATEFUGUE

This is what I hate.
I hate that the bullies & thugs of the world
who wound, damage, devastate others
are then by the dark magic of art
enshrined in the art of those others
who have survived, & whose survival is commemorated
in art; I hate that the suffering of victims
flowers into art, white helichrysums bravely enduring
in frost, through bleached rib cages.
And hateful the pride in survival, the words *victim,
survival*. And hateful the pride of triumph—
You did not murder us utterly, we are still here.
Are you surprised, some of us are still here?
And we will multiply!
I hate that pride, so small it fits into a Grimm's thimble.

I hate that Celan's great poem of the Holocaust,
"Death Fugue," flowers out of the dung heap of the dead
& could not have come into being otherwise.
I hate the necessity of art that is compensatory
for such evil.
I hate the very triumph of such art that would suggest
the horror is not absolute, for such art
has flowered from it.
I hate the meager survivals,

the crushed straw through which the drowning man breathes,
and such gratitude in such breathing
through the crushed straw. I hate
the dirges, the dances on broken feet,
the sound of shattering glass
that is the voice of defiance in sorrow.
I hate the fact of it that is irremediable,
and I hate the history that enshrines the fact.
I hate this *having to pay such rapt attention to the bullies & thugs.*
I hate how they continue to command our attention,
I hate that the greatest revenge seems to be beyond us—
to erase, to forget. To obliterate the memory of such evil,
the swastika, the silly mustache commanding
the marching men, smokestacks and empty skies,
the swagger of the bully, the mean smile of murder,
the swill of evil,
the smells.
I hate that the great art that has flowered from such carrion,
yet carries the whiff of carrion, the terror of the victims,
the suffering of the innocent that never ceases,
and the *bearing witness* that must never cease—
I hate that such knowing annuls all possibility
of not-knowing.
And most, I hate that the bullies & thugs are the prime movers,
whose polished boots set all into motion,
swinging pendulum that never ceases
once set
into motion.

A DREAM OF STOPPED-UP DRAINS

Köln, Germany
6 September 1977

1.

And then we came to the cathedral city of Köln on the wide Rhine
River.
Never before had we come to the cathedral city of Köln on the wide
    Rhine River.
In drumming rain the great Baroque cathedral rose over the rebuilt
    city of Köln on the wide Rhine River.
"Look!"—but no matter how high you cast your eyes
    you could not see the tops of the twin spires
    of the great Baroque cathedral at Köln.

In the drumming rain, a sharp smell of drains in the cathedral city
of Köln.
The ruins of the medieval city rebuilt on the wide Rhine River.
The great Baroque cathedral alone had been spared from Allied
bombing.
So God protects His own churchmen, sometimes.
So God stoops to intervene in the affairs of men.
So God in His caprice selects who will live, who will die
    at the time God selects, and no other.

Across the vast cathedral square of drumming rain and milling tourists
    there arose the wish to believe in the God
    of the great Baroque cathedral at Köln.

In our hotel room, top floor of the newly constructed Königshof,
    a view from every window of the great Baroque cathedral of Köln
    and a smell of backed-up drains.
In the bathroom amid the bright glittering tile, a smell of backed-up drains.
"Look!"—for in the tile floor near the sink, a drain measuring
    approximately nine inches in circumference.
An open metal drain through which you could see dark water churning.
Dark water flecked with foam, or froth. In which something swam.
Unless it was vibrations?—we stared, we could not see.
A powerful smell rose from the drain.
A smell of time, a smell of anguish, a smell of spilt brains, a smell of
    blue gas, a smell of raw life prevailing through time.
God is this power of raw, prevailing life.

A six-foot blond woman from the Königshof front desk came bringing
    Buz Fresh aerosol and disinfectant and a deft whisk brush.
Brisk sound of faucets, toilet flushing. And again flushing.
(How the heart sinks, a toilet twice flushed!)
Perhaps something was retrieved from the drain for safekeeping, or
    perhaps it was flushed away into oblivion.
No records are kept at the Königshof.

"I am very sorry, these things happen."
The air was lavishly sprayed, a pungent flower scent. Out of the dark
    German forest, sudden aroma of white lilies!

Carefully we placed the Köln telephone book over the drain.
A smell of stopped-up drains prevailed in the cathedral city of Köln
    On the wide Rhine River, but we could no longer smell it.

I had journeyed to Köln to give a public appearance.
It was my duty in Köln to present myself in words.
Yet we were in a desolate rural area.
We had been brought here, to be taken elsewhere.
Along a road, a truck with a dented fender moved toward us.
The driver stopped. He spoke only German, a burly man with
    strong hands and a close-shaved head.
His face was broad, frank and honest, modeled like a clay head.
His eyes shone flatly like polished glass.
Here was no man of mere language but a man of the soil.
Here was no man of mere poetry but a man of the people.
Here was a man upon whom the state could depend.
He would bring me to my public appearance
    except I was not prepared.
I had misplaced my material, I had no words in any language!
That flimsy life raft upon which I had imagined I might survive.
How quickly and shamefully I spoke. Yet there was defiance
    in my voice.
I heard myself declare: Yes. I am partly Jewish.
My family was Hungarian on my mother's side, and Irish and
German
    Jewish on my father's side.

My German-Jewish great-grandparents had emigrated to upstate
    New York in the late 1890s. They'd settled in northern Niagara
    County. They'd changed their name from Morgenstern to
    Morningstar, wishing to become American.

These remote facts I explained to the driver.
I had nothing to provide except my history.
I thought—*But I am not my history, am I?*
I thought—*But I am free of time, aren't I?*
Seeing the driver's strong hands, I became agitated.
The man was working-class, his nails were blunt and edged with
dirt.
He knew nothing of poetry, of subtlety and subterfuge.
He knew nothing of my public identity, his instinct was unerring.
We were in such a desolate place!
What facts are there in history except *which place? Which time?*
I was uttering words I had not ever uttered in any language.
"Please hold me, please be kind to me."
My ancestors spoke, through the gritty soil stuffed into their
mouths.
The man's strong fingers were stroking and caressing my head.
Here was the simulation of protectiveness as when a father,
    his thoughts distracted, takes time to comfort a frightened child.
The driver stroked my shoulders, my arms.
I was only a child, I began to cry.
I was very frightened as only children in their wisdom can be
frightened.
This is my dream!–yet I could not prevent what would come next.
I thought—*I must behave with dignity.*

How surprised I would have been in my former life to see
　　myself on my knees in this desolate wooded place!
The landscape was foreign like the language.
The soil was rough, though sandy.
The sky was the hue of wet, wadded newsprint.
The wind smelled faintly of stopped-up drains.
At a horizon, the sun glowed like a hot coin.
The sun was a word for *elsewhere,* and *another time.*
When you turned to the sun for more light the sun faded,
　　like the fall into sleep.

On my knees I hid my face. I wasn't crying, I think.
The driver closed his strong fingers around my neck and
　　began to squeeze, grunting with effort.
Death by manual strangulation. Which was not common.

To be strangled is a terrible way to die, but
　　I was not there for it.

BLOODLINE, ELEGY: *Su Qijian Family, Beijing*

In the mud-colored Hai River a swirl of infant-girl bodies.
In the river-trance the infant girls are propelled with the current.
You stare, you blink—she has vanished.
But—here is another, and
soon, another.
How small, how fleeting, of no more consequence than a kitten
an infant girl drowned at birth
before the first breath has been drawn, and expelled—
No crying. We do not shatter the peace of the morning, with crying.
See how good we are!

In the mud-river so many, you could not count how many.
Out of the bloody womb the small bodies betray the infant girls
for they are revealed incomplete between the legs, pitiable
the *not-male*, the doomed.

We have not been drowned in the Hai River for we
are of the privileged Su Qijian family. And yet
our dreams are filled with drowning amid the swirl
of infant-girl bodies in the Hai River
sweeping past our home.
We do not want to know how the infant girls are our sisters or our
aunts.

We do not want to know how they are us, for (it is said) they are not us, that is all we have been told.
And we did not see these infant-girl bodies in the swirl of the mud-river, for we had not yet been born.

We are the largest family in Beijing. We are very proud to be of the Su Qijian family of Beijing. We have been chosen for the honor of meeting you today because we are a perfect family (it is said), for we have been born and our baby girls not drowned. *Bloodline* is all, and in our bloodline it is a marvel, it is a source of great pride, how our mother, our grandmothers, our great-grandmothers had not been thrown into the mud-river to drown but were allowed to live.

So we know, we are blessed! We are very special amid so many millions drowned in the Hai River as in the great Yangtze and how many millions perished in the Revolution of no more consequence than infant girls extinguished before they can draw breath or cry.

Especially, we do not cry.
We have never cried.
You will not hear us cry—*See how good we are! Even in the agony of death, our tiny lungs filled with the mud-river.*

We of the Su Qijian family have never lamented or mourned for our privilege is to have been allowed to be born.
We are alive, there are twenty-nine of us alive and not one of us has been drowned at birth. So we are blessed, we are of the People's Republic of China. We are alive.

For some Chinese couples just one baby was allowed. For some
others, more than one baby was allowed. And for some, girl babies
were allowed. We do not understand these decrees,
and we do not question.

Bloodline is the very god. Bloodline is the nation.
Bloodline is property of the Office of China State Council
Information.

And then in a dream it is revealed—
it is the mothers of our family who drowned our sisters!

Long ago it happened, in those years
before we were born. It was a different China then (it is said),
it is not the same China now. Our beautiful mother
pleads for understanding. All our mothers weep and tear their hair
in shame! They would tear out their eyes that such ugliness
might spare them.

How is it possible, our mothers are those very mothers
who tossed the infant girls into the river to drown . . .
Oh, but it happened long ago. The world was different then.
Shuxia is saying, Junxia is saying, Lixia is saying,
they are not evil. Not one of the women of the Su Qijian family
is evil, they plead with us to understand, and to forgive.
Our babies who are your sisters were torn from our arms,
we could not nurse them, we were forbidden. *You see,
we had no choice. We are but
female, we had no choice but to drown our own.*

It is China thrumming with its many millions that is alive,
that is the marvel. In the distance you see the eye of our god
the China Central Television Tower, rising above the suety Beijing
skyline, that is a greater marvel. *Rejoice! Our great nation
is the future, and your nation is of the past.*

What is the meaning of our lives, we never ask.
The creatures of the hive do not question the hive.
The creatures of the river that do not drown
in the river do not question the river, for the river
has spared them, and that is the blessing. This is the meaning
of all of our lives, and not just Chinese lives.
That we are is the meaning, and that we have been blessed
is the meaning, and that we are not drowned
in the Hai River with our infant sisters is the meaning.

In parting here is our gift to you, our American visitors: a plastic
bag of photographs of Chinese monuments, Chinese citizens, the
mud-colored Hai River at dawn when it glitters with light like the
scales of a great serpent whose head you cannot see thousands of
miles upstream, and whose tail you cannot see thousands of miles
downstream, that abides forever.

HARVESTING SKIN

> The skin is the largest organ in the
> body. The skin of an average-sized
> man has an area of approximately
> 17 square feet and weighs about 5
> pounds.
> —*medical handbook*

Fast & unfaltering to remove skin
from the dead & soon-to-be
is a delicate task.

Few physicians are qualified.
You must have advanced degrees
in human-tissue studies & (of course)
surgery. I'd
begun at twenty-
one.

Burn-unit specialist is my title.
You see me on the scene at executions, I
am booked weeks in advance.

Harvesting (human) skin
requires a steady hand & eye
& I take pride in customers
satisfied.

For skin is a body-commodity.
We seek skin, kidneys, liver, heart,
bones, corneas—
for *research*.

In fact these are for sale.
I am not a salesman but a supplier.
Our skin is sold to customers by
the square centimeter.

What's our price? Depends
upon the quality of the skin.
If torn, mutilated, bruised, etc.
If perfect, it's expensive.
And all depends
(you know this)
upon the Market.

(What is the Market, no
one knows. Ever-shifting
as the tide our God
cannot be worshipped,
only just supplied.)

At twenty-one
so young,
my hand shook. Forty
minutes to an hour & still the job
was often bungled & the harvest
cheaply sold.

Now I am experienced. I am
skilled. Ten to twenty minutes
after the condemned is killed
is all I require, &
ten harvestings per day
is not unusual.

Swift incisions into the dermis.
Swift peelings. Swift removal.
On ice the commodity is placed
& rushed to skin-graft artists
& their patients.

Our prices are high, only wealthy
customers can buy.
All benefit: burn, cancer, injury &
cosmetic patients, & the condemned
who are spared lifetime in prison.

(This season, between arrest
& harvest
as brief as 48 hours!)

After skin, organs & bones & corneas
are harvested, what remains
is cleanly burnt.

The donor does not know the recipient
of his skin. The donor does not (sometimes)
know that he is to die.
For why

such knowledge,
lacking power?
Yet his skin embraces the recipient.
As an eyeball in an eye
Socket, & blood
Embraced by blood.

The old way was wasteful, so
much skin unharvested.
Our new way is cruel
you will say. But when
you require skin,
you will bargain,
and you will buy.

(The speaker is a former doctor at a Chinese People's Liberation Army
Hospital, Beijing.)

"THIS IS THE TIME FOR WHICH WE HAVE BEEN WAITING"

Dear Jim,

I *finally got your letter enclosing your letter enclocussing your letter which was so ompportant foe me, thannkuok yuon very much. In time this fainful bsiness will soonfeul will soon be onert. Tnany anany goodness. If S lossiee eii wyyonor wy sinfaignature.

I hope I hope I make it.

**Bill
(handwritten signature)**

The first snowfall brings chaos.
First the horizon disappears then
you disappear. When

William Carlos Williams suffered his first stroke
he was sixty-eight years old, in 1951. His second,
the following year. No man more loved

our American speech. Vulgar & graceless
as oversized boots he loved it. The pimply-
faced girl he loved. Forms inside things gnarly

to the touch. Smokestacks belching flame, mustard
weed, chain-link fencing. Steely river seething with acid
& sparrows picking in the dirt, like Death. Yet

still just sparrows. Coarse beauty of nasturtiums,
& fried oysters. Beauty of spiderwebs,
Brueghel's hunters in the snow. Except

maybe the physician saw & heard too much!
Maybe what the poet saw & heard
was in his own head! Maybe in Rutherford,
N.J., there was nothing. Maybe

the poet was in despair, fierce lover
Of women & adulterer & this morning waking to discover
Someone has dressed him in an old man's underwear—

gunmetal-gray, woolen-itchy, soiled cuffs
at bony wrists & ankles & the crotch unsnapped.
Opens his mouth to curse

& words choke like phlegm. A doctor doesn't expect
to die like the rest of us . . . Waking in the sun
in Flossie's garden back of the yellow house

the terror strikes him maybe he's dreamt it all?—male
hands lifting a thrashing bloody infant
from behind female thighs, &

ironweed along the railroad embankment
tough enough to thrive in cinders, &
there he's laughing typing on the old Underwood manual

words leaping astonished out of the mute keyboard, keys
so worn you can't read the letters. And
those clouds—

clouds I've been noticing this morning, too.
Diesel-dirtied, broken & yet dignified in motion
moving from west to east effortless above the pines

In this New Jersey smudged air. In March 1963
the final stroke. "Died in his sleep." Eyes
moving restlessly down the naked body.

On a gurney? Since when? The shock of it, his young
male body restored. Svelte dark down of the chest,
groin and soft stirring penis. Winter-pale

haunches, muscles hard as bone. Lifts
his head. Where? Christ, he's alert, he's curious—
God-damned ready to begin it all again—

This is the time for which we have been waiting.

Note: The letter from William Carlos Williams to his friend and
editor James Laughlin was written sometime shortly prior to June 1962, when
Williams's last book, *Pictures from Brueghel and Other Poems*, was published.

THE TUNNEL

Early April, descending
the long broken hill
behind Panoramic Way.

Morning radioactive-bright.
The hill a puzzle of concrete outcroppings
broken and discontinuous as the aphorisms of Nietzsche.

And the Tunnel not (yet) visible
though its peristalsis begins
to pull, squeeze, tug.

In the dazzling distance,
San Francisco Bay.
As you descend the hill

the glittering Bay retreats
like a memory of happiness
but still

the palette is wide, seemingly random
in sunshine like spangled coins
the curious uneven descent

like a drunk
staggering
and the Tunnel not (yet)

defined as in a canvas
of Magritte where it's the absence of
depth that assures

This is art, not life.
This will not hurt you.

And now passing
the abandoned house
gigantic, stucco

strangely surrounded by chain-link fencing,
razor wire absurd in swagger
protecting what no one wants.
And still you descend the hill
bravely, boldly
blindly seeing now

the deserted playing field,
deserted playground.
Stilled swings, rusted slide

O where has life gone?—
abandoning these places
abruptly at Warring Street,

and then to Derby
more rapidly now
the Tunnel narrows

at Stuart, College, Russell too
swiftly passing way-stations
of ordinary life

you would clutch at, in
your descent
except sucked by peristalsis

tugged past, breathless
and now the sky lowered
like a sound-proofed ceiling

unremitting, no mercy
at Ashby Avenue
rudely tugged as a teat

made to turn right onto Ashby,
as the morning shudders
visibly, you can feel shrinkage

as out of pastel treetops
the Hospital emerges
grim in efficiency

the "boundless" sky
has vanished, at the Hospital
driveway in the grip

of peristalsis tugged
through the automatic doors
in whose glass a frightened face

appears, disappears
and into the twilit foyer
and to the double elevators

rising inexorably to the sixth floor
to room 765
where your life awaits you

sleeping, a tube in his bruised nose
clasped hands on the distended belly
breathing in random gusts

like the lone wind at shore,
and a sickle moon above.

O Love—where will you abide when our frail bodies are no more?

PALLIATIVE

1.

Hate hope!
Arsenic for weeks
we'd taken in micro-drops
on credulous tongues.

Hope the thing
with noisome wings
clattering
about our heads
with a broom at last swatted to earth.
Stomped, smashed.

Now, clarity of silence.
Only the drip of minimal liquids—saline, Dilaudid.
Only the labored and arrhythmic breathing
as the chest rises, falls—rises,
falls.
Faintest of echoes—*Give up on.*

2.

Hold desperation
like a playing card
close to the heart
reluctant to reveal
what you feel
but (yes) you risk
the irrevocable loss
too late.

And so on the brink of *too late*
(when no one else is in the room)
(for a hospice room can be crowded)
(by "crowded" meaning more than two people)
you tell your husband that you love him
so much, what a wonderful
husband he has been
and he says—*But I failed you by dying.*
And you protest—*But why are you saying*
such a thing, you are not
dying, we are talking
Here together!—
And he says *Because I am dead.*

As after the final biopsy
he'd been incensed—*They took my soul from me.*
They took me to the crematorium, I saw the sign.
Don't try to tell me I didn't see the sign.

3.

Trapped in this bed like a prison.
Is the car out front? Drive the car around.
Where are the keys to the car?
Joyce, don't leave. Joyce?
We need to get the car. Where are the keys . . .
I want to go home. Take me home. Joyce—
don't leave me!
What did we do with the car?

4.

In hospice time ceases.
Hours lapse into days
and days into night
and again day, and
night and the mouth
once fierce in kissing
and being kissed
is slack, mute.
And breathing slows,
asymmetrical
as a listing boat.
And fever dreams rage
beneath bluish eyelids
quivering in secret life.
Until at last the deepest sigh
of a lifetime . . .

5.

After such struggle
you must love
the unrippled dark
water in which
the perfect cold O
of the moon floats

ACKNOWLEDGMENTS

I am grateful to my poet-friends Henri Cole and the late C. K. Williams for having read many of these poems in manuscript, and for their overall generosity and encouragement; and to my dear late husband Charlie Gross for his hope that I would gather the poems into a volume.

Much gratitude and thanks are also due to the editors of those magazines in which most of these poems appeared, which include *New Yorker* ("Harlow's Monkeys"; "In Hemp-Woven Hammocks Reading the *Nation*," under the title, "This Is the Season"; "Edward Hopper's 'Eleven A.M.,' 1926"; "Too Young to Marry but Not Too Young to Die"; "Jubilate: An Homage in Catterel Verse" (*New Yorker* online); *New York Review of Books* ("Exsanguination," "Loney"); *Poetry* ("Little Albert, 1920," "The Coming Storm," "The First Room," "Sinkholes," "That Other," "The Blessing," "American Sign Language"); *Atlantic* ("Apocalypso"); *Salmagundi* ("Hometown"; "To Marlon Brando in Hell," "Old America Has Come Home to Die," "The Tunnel," "Palliative"); *Paris Review* ("The Mercy," "Harvesting Skin"); *Boulevard* ("Doctor Help Me"); *New Republic* ("Hatefugue"); *Kenyon Review* ("Bloodline, Elegy"); *Yale Review* ("A Dream of Stopped-Up Drains").

"Kite Poem" was included by Robert Pinsky in a *Slate* (online) poetry project (2003) and "This Is the Time for Which We Have Been Waiting" was included in *Visiting Dr. Williams: Poems Inspired By the Life and Work of William Carlos Williams,* ed. Sheila Coghill and Thom Tammaro (2011). "To Marlon Brando in Hell" was included in *The Best American Poetry 2017,* ed. Natasha Trethewey and David Lehman.

Photo credit: Charlie Gross, Lake George, 2018.